PIANO SOLO

STAR TREK
INTO DARKNESS

ISBN 978-1-4803-5285-8

HAL•LEONARD®
CORPORATION

7777 W. BLUEMOUND RD. P.O. BOX 13819 MILWAUKEE, WI 53213

In Australia Contact:
Hal Leonard Australia Pty. Ltd.
4 Lentara Court
Cheltenham, Victoria, 3192 Australia
Email: ausadmin@halleonard.com.au

For all works contained herein:
Unauthorized copying, arranging, adapting, recording, Internet posting, public performance,
or other distribution of the printed music in this publication is an infringement of copyright.
Infringers are liable under the law.

Visit Hal Leonard Online at
www.halleonard.com

SUB PRIME DIRECTIVE

Written by MICHAEL GIACCHINO

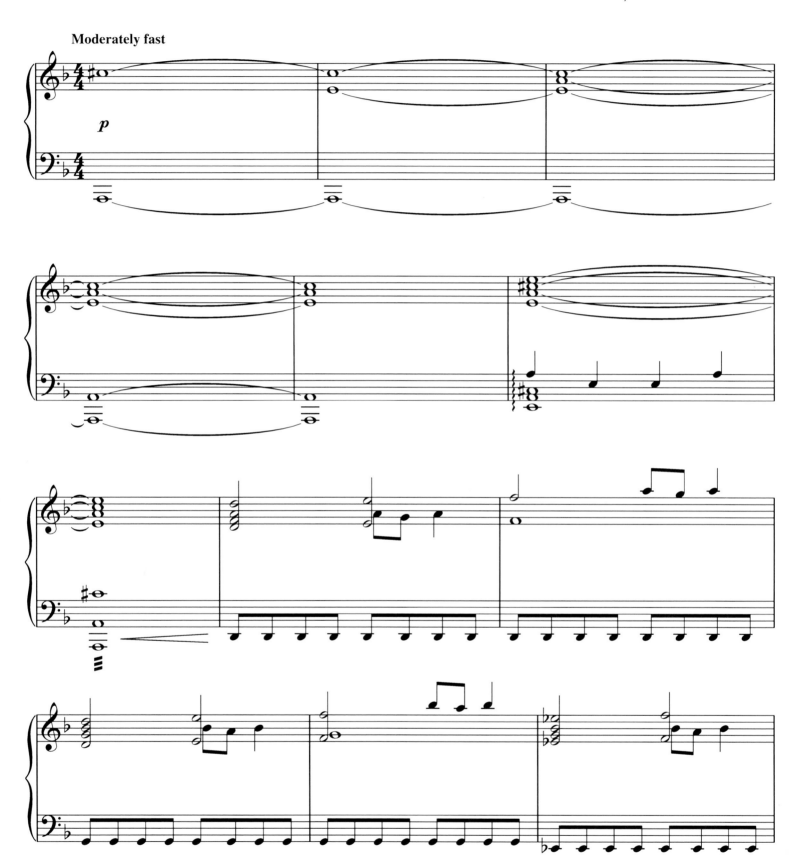

Contains Portions of the TV Theme by Alexander Courage and Gene Roddenberry
Copyright © 2013 Paramount Pictures Corporation d/b/a Paramount Allegra Music
All Rights Administered by Sony/ATV Harmony, 8 Music Square West, Nashville, TN 37203
International Copyright Secured   All Rights Reserved
Star Trek Theme
Written by Alexander Courage and Gene Roddenberry
Copyright © 1966, 1970 (Renewed 1994, 1998) Bruin Music Company
All Rights Administered by Sony/ATV Melody, 8 Music Square West, Nashville, TN 37203
International Copyright Secured   All Rights Reserved

6

MELD-MERIZED

Written by MICHAEL GIACCHINO

Moderately slow

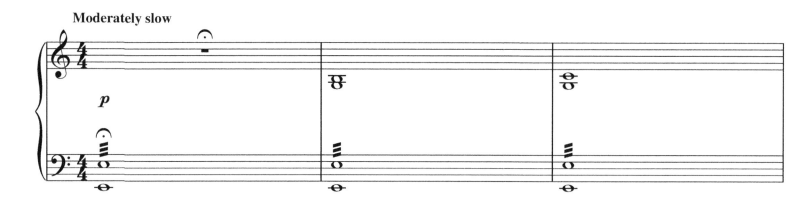

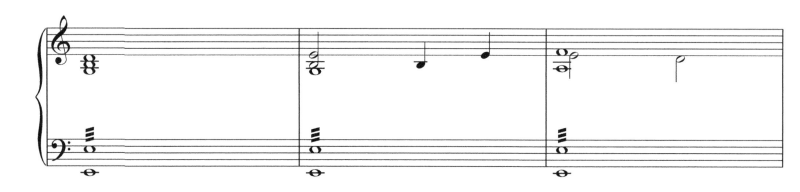

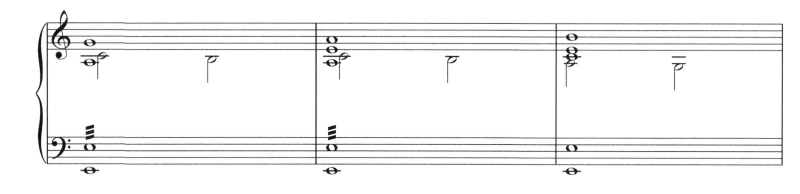

Copyright © 2013 Paramount Pictures Corporation d/b/a Paramount Allegra Music
All Rights Administered by Sony/ATV Harmony, 8 Music Square West, Nashville, TN 37203
International Copyright Secured   All Rights Reserved

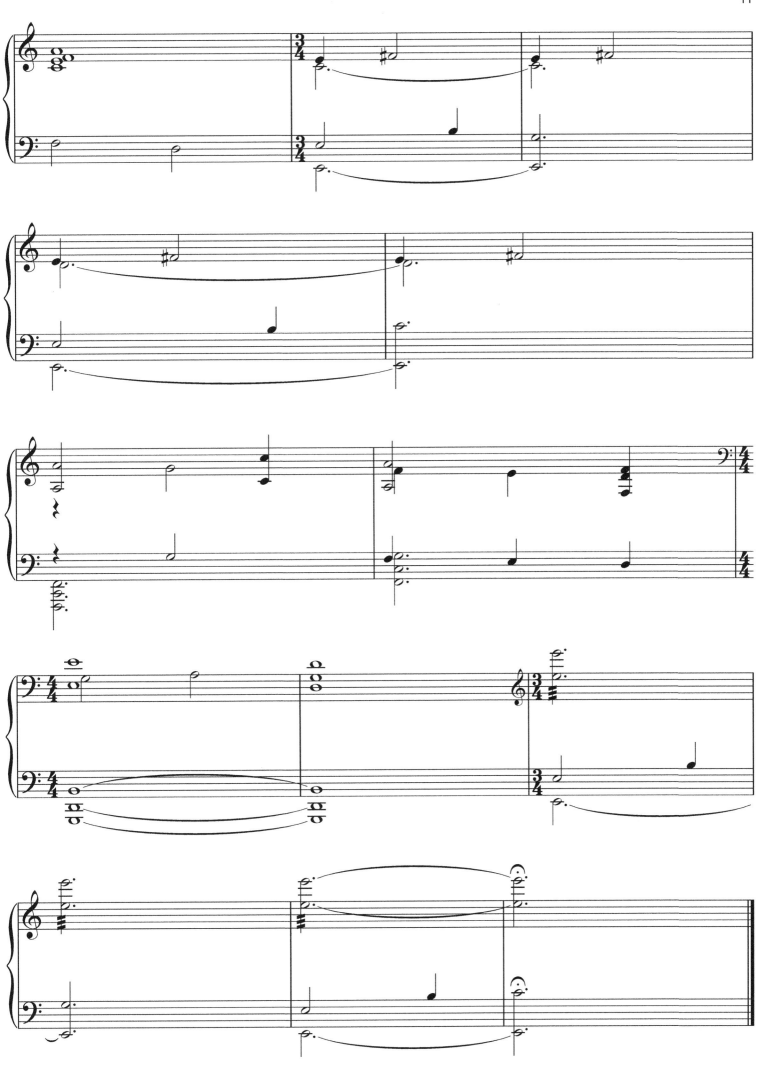

LONDON CALLING

Written by MICHAEL GIACCHINO

Moderately, in 2

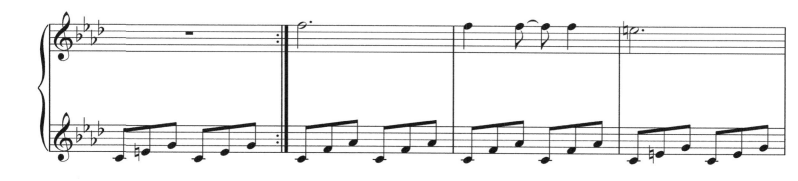

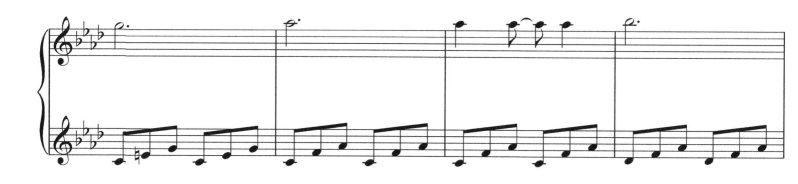

Copyright © 2013 Paramount Pictures Corporation d/b/a Paramount Allegra Music
All Rights Administered by Sony/ATV Harmony, 8 Music Square West, Nashville, TN 37203
International Copyright Secured   All Rights Reserved

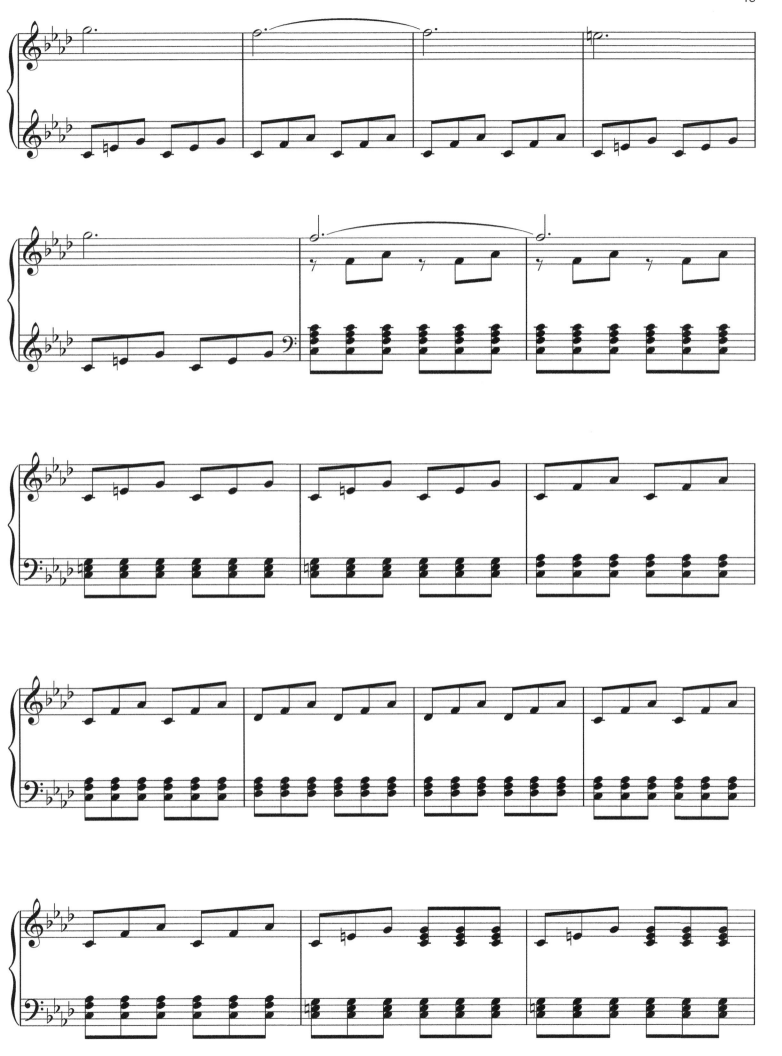

BRIGADOOM

Written by MICHAEL GIACCHINO

Copyright © 2013 Paramount Pictures Corporation d/b/a Paramount Allegra Music
All Rights Administered by Sony/ATV Harmony, 8 Music Square West, Nashville, TN 37203
International Copyright Secured   All Rights Reserved

Half as fast (♩ = ♪)

Moderately, in 2

WARP CORE VALUES

Written by MICHAEL GIACCHINO

Copyright © 2013 Paramount Pictures Corporation d/b/a Paramount Allegra Music
All Rights Administered by Sony/ATV Harmony, 8 Music Square West, Nashville, TN 37203
International Copyright Secured   All Rights Reserved

22

Moderately fast

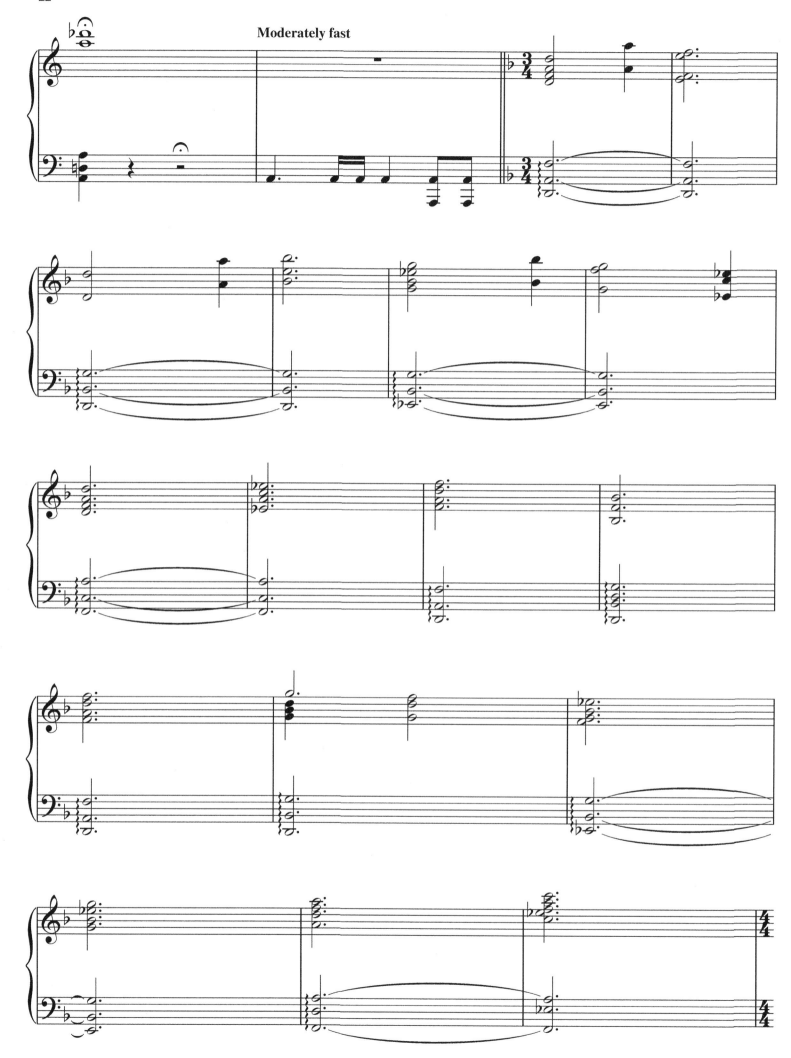

BUYING THE SPACE FARM

Written by MICHAEL GIACCHINO

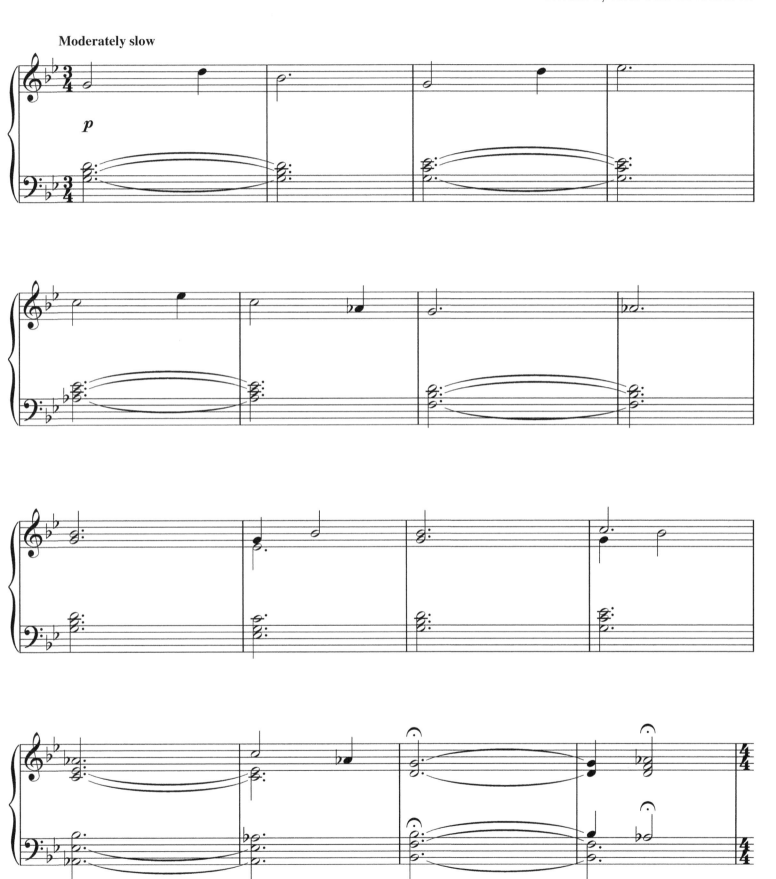

Copyright © 2013 Paramount Pictures Corporation d/b/a Paramount Allegra Music
All Rights Administered by Sony/ATV Harmony, 8 Music Square West, Nashville, TN 37203
International Copyright Secured   All Rights Reserved

KIRK ENTERPRISES

Written by MICHAEL GIACCHINO

Contains Portions of the TV Theme by Alexander Courage and Gene Roddenberry
Copyright © 2013 Paramount Pictures Corporation d/b/a Paramount Allegra Music
All Rights Administered by Sony/ATV Harmony, 8 Music Square West, Nashville, TN 37203
International Copyright Secured   All Rights Reserved
Star Trek Theme
Written by Alexander Courage and Gene Roddenberry
Copyright © 1966, 1970 (Renewed 1994, 1998) Bruin Music Company
All Rights Administered by Sony/ATV Melody, 8 Music Square West, Nashville, TN 37203
International Copyright Secured   All Rights Reserved

Tempo I

Moderately fast

rall.

STAR TREK MAIN THEME

Written by MICHAEL GIACCHINO

Contains Portions of the TV Theme by Alexander Courage and Gene Roddenberry
Copyright © 2013 Paramount Pictures Corporation d/b/a Paramount Allegra Music
All Rights Administered by Sony/ATV Harmony, 8 Music Square West, Nashville, TN 37203
International Copyright Secured   All Rights Reserved
Star Trek Theme
Written by Alexander Courage and Gene Roddenberry
Copyright © 1966, 1970 (Renewed 1994, 1998) Bruin Music Company
All Rights Administered by Sony/ATV Melody, 8 Music Square West, Nashville, TN 37203
International Copyright Secured   All Rights Reserved